Pitch & Glint

Pitch & Glint

Lutz Seiler

*Translated from the
German by Stefan Tobler*

SHEFFIELD – LONDON – NEW YORK

First published in English translation in 2023 by And Other Stories
Sheffield – London – New York
www.andotherstories.org

© Suhrkamp Verlag Frankfurt am Main 2000
First published as *pech & blende* in 2000.
All rights reserved by and controlled through Suhrkamp Verlag Berlin.
Translation and afterword copyright © Stefan Tobler, 2023

1 3 5 7 9 8 6 4 2

Print ISBN: 9781913505769
eBook ISBN: 9781913505776

Editor: Tara Tobler; Copy-editor: Robina Pelham Burn; Proofreader: Sarah Terry;
Typesetter: Tetragon, London; Typefaces: Albertan Pro and Linotype Syntax (interior)
and Stellage (cover); Series Cover Design: Elisa von Randow, Alles Blau Studio,
Brazil, after a concept by And Other Stories; Author Photo: Renate von Mangoldt.

Grateful acknowledgement is made to the following, in which some of these
translations first appeared: *Modern Poetry in Translation*, *New Statesman*, *PN Review*,
PROTOTYPE, *Shearsman*, *Sheffield Telegraph*, the *TLS* and *Wet Grain*.

And Other Stories books are printed and bound in the UK on FSC-certified
paper by Clays Ltd. The covers are of G . F Smith 270gsm Colorplan
card, which is sustainably manufactured at the James Cropper paper
mill in the Lake District, and are stamped with biodegradable foil.

And Other Stories gratefully acknowledges that its work is supported
using public funding by Arts Council England and the translation of
this book was supported by a grant from the Goethe-Institut.

CONTENTS

Everyone has only one song.

PAUL BOWLES

I

mechanics of the pictorial world

taking down the swing
in autumn & putting it up
in April. day after day

the suburb commutes under
the trees and hour after hour
from the sky above courtyards

pulverised swallows fall & neatly
stuffed ones come up: the
gravity in their eyes hangs

raw as an egg
over the globe over
the man at the next table

(in sleep he leans his face
against the lamp) and over
the slender animals here

that each evening
creep down the avenue
& murmur

ev'nin into the dark as
if tucking the greeting away
in their warm almost

sleeping bodies

latrine

once, it was said, the root of her cough
shone down the narrow
stairs on us, feeble children
   with cold
   piss, butcher's grandchildren in the night, who

loved the light in the radio & the clockwork's
proclamations, eiderdown kids, steaming
   birds, all that had been
her house, her tiredness too, if
it rained, was that the courtyard and that
the dog and
   it was the butcher's rope with

mother quiet   the vertebrae
cracked apart, I was still
standing in the kitchen
behind her cupboard
and didn't know if,
where I was, I could ever
be found again or
if I was already dead or was it
the others outside who had died
mother, father, Gagarin & Heike or

mother ahead standing ready not quiet
too tired for the humidity in the air &
her hand raised, as if
the animal was wanting
   one last time to be

soothed by her, and yet
she had done that too and
had become even more lonely
   with the road to the pass at her back
   a bread van in the courtyard, the
   opening & closing of tears . . .

there was a kinship between our houses

there were ducks on duckweed
and, miss, your seamstressing
between the silver heads of willows, there was

your basil laugh with sewing machine
with measuring tape and a couple of dummies. what
was there to laugh about? there was

nothing to laugh about, there was, sorry,
also nothing to talk about, there
were ducks on duckweed

and, miss, your *seamstressing*

fin de siècle

I walked through snow with all the nervous
post-war whip-cracked lamps behind my neck
across Vienna's Mozart bridge and there
a tired Irish setter was still sitting
   tethered he

was dead and waiting for me
I mean I untied his rope
from the railing base and began
to swing the creature a little
to and fro *skin & bony light*
the bells are ringing a flurry of snow
   started I sang

a little song about the Danube over
and over (I was a child) the dead
setter circled now at the end
of my arm above the lovely
balustrade he curved
light and large into the nervous
post-war lamplight a rip
widened at his throat a whistling

got up and the rigid
skins on his eyes clicked
tiredly open and closed: oh, you'd

have loved the mechanics of the blink
and would have been lonelier still
above the snow, the bridge & the old song

Greater Berlin, one

the smell of the last allotments & heavy
lifting at the huts: some
            hung sleigh bells on
pockets bulky and hard, late-
returning POWs' greatcoats, we
still had tinsel, net curtains in
the cherry trees, bottles, wherever you stepped, onto
            their short, brown necks. there

            we perched at the table with splayed-
out partings, a couple of
pounds of puppies under eyelids: lattice
fences, asbestos roofs 4ever or
some he-won't-bite pit bull in the pimps'
            racket & crystal-

            clear bottles, first off heavy
and hard to let go, then empty
buried in rats'
            holes, their necks whistling

towards the Western moon. how good
that rat-bashing felt in the
            northwester & what
we here now always have: this

patrolling beyond the tips of the skull, by day
when reverie carefully beds its temples
in layers of air, raw
nerves on bark, on cortex, when

in early light the head
& life of a bird smack
into each other

spoilheap glow

we're talking physics here: incidents, apparent lifelessness,
mineshaft temples suddenly purple; *spoilheap glow*
was a drinkable liquor, duty-free
                    for cave-dwellers, but:
'on Labour Day, out on the street'.

                    and evenings
the acrylic jacket, in the stalls
for stone-age operettas, cattle
in the outbuilding, evenings
the Easter bunny's twitching; a bundle

hanging draughty on a beam compare
to rabbits, mange-eaten: when first
your feet lose their sight, then
the slow vanishing of your eyes; white

like how in my lamp's cone
survival leaps in
furs, furrows, down
country roads'
inner walls: you

   loved it when
the sheep undulated, their lousy
twitching in their sleep, the little
spasm in *Glück auf!* – it all

reminds you of something
under shavings, under-
mined a wind

at eye level
rises out of the past; with every look
the sides are changing, every blink is digging
    you a cave in time

scissors knives and matches

I was walking up to my knees with the current, so
corpses overtook me, a soft
white shoulder bashed
horizontal into the taut
throat of my knee I swayed forward,

side, together, tap with a water
waltzing step to let
a great dead swimmer slip
lengthwise past me but straight
away another water-head
was pushing between my legs, so

I stumbled, I did, no, not quite
I danced that next
quarter twist of my leg to the left,
back, side, together, tap
the dead, their way free, continued
stiff as pigs who swim between islands
down the boulevard, where to, I

don't know, it was raining I was dancing in
the giant heaving swell until
the evening threw down a shimmer for scissors
knives and matches
under thinly glazed fontanelles

Felizetti's garden

walking falls ill
with darkened grounds
& water from laughter & whistling
like crying like phlegm
on teeth plaque broken sentences
pierced ears I hate

the woman her hand on her eyes
brings the dark safely over
 down into her over-dark breath
 through the fencing

around our garden her weathered child
drifts with stones in his blood with
bird crap of hair tufts of
 the sheer stench over the garden
fence against the Felizetti

house stones and curses
smashed, the roof the
child jumps over & splits like
ice on pig bellies
 his spitty breath
tolls out in winter to the furnaces
in the villages' sky, utterly damned

you leave, Felizetti,
from our shame half a sentence
  half a child
with sugared lips you

    step into the tent of light above
the fields into the public body
of the forest a *magic pop-up lark* but

whatever in the root shadow of your trip
we kicked from your heels old Felizetti
whirled straight up to God

summing up

   you stand like a branch
your steps all wooden
   since the age of short trousers
in the shadow: a third one.

   a forward bend
it finds its place
   at a quicker pace

it rises up
   it passes soon
going down the road. only a sudden

   staticky hiss
whatever the frequency
so not with standing
you lean into your steps

II

in the East, Lisa Rothe

were there people who
when coughing would completely
cover their face and vanish: Lisa Rothe, what
    we found in the drawer by her bed was enough
    for her feet's insect blackness
    refill for the footed lamps
in the snow, oil and phlegm, so that's

where she kept the light, the elements
of the mirror, we threw up, we found
the impression of a sleeping head &
her faeces, water and quiet

remarks about us, the potatoes
ticking in the pantries, *the inner paddock*, that's
    how she'd shrunk below the noises
    of a street, of a stream, of a

Wismut works stadium, that's
    how she'd gone dark
    in the spotlight of her desk lamp, slipped
      like soft food,
solid food, until you fall asleep, soft food, solid . . . we

    ourselves had turned the bedcovers
far back *out of the snow*
    washed cheekbones, mistle-blood . . . but
we bore the smell, the personal

infections, *a*
dance teacher from an eastern suburb
slower than mandrake, gave birth . . . no
there's not a thing to hear, there's

really not a single thing
to hear, the quiet potted
meat beside
  her makeshift posture &

  well-kempt sleep, it's
September now
and beasts are creeping
in, nothing's lacking

what remains remains

first you smell the flagellated
table legs out front
of the palazzi the good

poems stroll home
& through wide
eyes cut out of paper

drink to your dream, a glass
in which you wave you
have waved and

must wave on and on not a
speedy steam-ahead but a steady dead
waving of your hand as part of your hand as

a great white carved out of the face
eye at the height
of the stands

on the sheep track

April; I collected strides on steps
of stone, I touched & drank
the breath in the ditches the cold

echo sprung from my temples *once*
in a never, a weak return
is a squeak of a sigh: what

occurs is misted
by the spittle of birds the ear
asleep in oil the dead grow

& die in the garden, silence
is a vertical sleep

for Jan Skácel

the sixth blue black August

but I'd seen how she had stood
there, so small, on the beach
and nameless

so what's your name
your name's how you've
always walked snow
in the evening absorbed in handiwork. unbelievable how
under your fingertips the piano begins. what was
your mother called, slow bird? all dining room, all slender
heart? and what was your father called under the lamp, how do you
look out, what do you look like, maybe a forgotten animal
speaks out of you, a bone
in the laughter of sheep? a hundred dogs buried without mounds
is time for a time, so what is your name?
don't you have milk duty? what are you looking for in the water?
rail-bridge phobia, a freezing skiff? there
is no skiff, there is a reef, a riff, there is time
how time whistles, for a time beautiful
how under your fingertips, the piano begins

for Dunja and Max

but it was good

   to breathe, out
& in went our breath on the sails
of our galleon-lamp, we had
its dark, mechanical light, we had albata
on the ashtray, and nails, alone
as Crusoe, crooked in slates, deep

in the radio slept the radio-child with
   tubes & relays, which it
alone understood, a cracking such
as big ships make, flashing a signal, something
   between out in the evenings, then silent
& quietly on again: alone

   in the dark came
the frequencies later never to be found, local
frequencies of ageing, the disappeared
   villages &
their weak chromosome strokes on
 the dials – I

saw Crusoe, my father; his
   baptism, timbers round his temples,
   back home he laughed, the man
with the beaming hand, his hissing, his
 crackling, they hear

how everything ends, slips, *two*
  legs the coastline the soft
  parting of feet in a stride

for Jürgen Becker

Berlin room

lights off, & click: the spyholes
in the doors and *once*
        words went through
the stairwells, places
that we hadn't heard of names
that we didn't know of from words, went

up & down. lights on, & fall:
mid-stride the walking
        crumbled crawled
with dragging foot went back
towards another century's
        room and through
a dad-cave of baccy & Activist

Worker's trophies down to
children's musty rooms and tiptoe past
ye olde bullseye glass the smell
        of Dear Departed Comrades:
the compass pricks & hammer hits
the hole cut in the flag

in the east of the land

wind came up the border
   dogs were rising on
their delicate branching skeletons

whistled a bewitching witless
wanderlied. the snow came in
& tore the iron

curtain of their eyes, a
blunted gaze towards the hinterland
made plain that we made do. and yes

we would have, if we could
have gone, stayed
   at home forever

the thing which blew at us from large, inhabited trees
was at home deep
in the time of conversations, tree talk
was tree cake and lay
heavy at home, like a bone at rest that had
as we kids often shouted been on its way
before your time, it had stridden across the fields

and breathed on them, and we had
long and happily known to praise it, we saw
that even our father loved it, called it
a *memory prop*, his heart's
signal box and the seed stock
of footsteps barely taken now, of crawler
vehicles, of ores and oils, broken from

his walking quarters, far beyond
the Culmitzsch dams, torn far from
a strange job near Selingstädt
with the Russian ores, their oils. and although
we should have long been asleep
we'd crowd down to mother, when father
went about at night and roared
       the bone the white was the bones
       with Russian oils and ores
as we said to ourselves, he smells the ore, it's the bone, yes

he'd climbed the spoilheaps
known the mines, the caterpillar tracks, the water, the schnapps
and so slid homewards, discoverer of the overburden,
we hear it ticking, it's the clock, it's
   his Geiger counter heart

where were you, Gagarin

in the end it's just
us standing here
again, holding good big
spoons in our hands, but

then we place
the eggs on the spoons
and carry
the spoons up the yard
to the coop and down
to Frau Koberski's room: and

if, yes, if our spoons
were to wobble, up
at the coop or down
at Frau Koberski's shore, if

the hostel wardens die,
the snowline sinks, if
the facts suggest
impending doom, we'll throw

a shaking foot out far
beyond the top field's cattle track
till Ronneburg, till Grossenstein,
till all around is falling down, falling down –

III

my class, born in sixty-three, that

       endless succession of children, a fixture
in the echo vault of the hallways, creeping
with a stoop into the pocket

of someone else's, unknown coat, seven
   full of wax with a heaviness
inhaled from floorboards, eight

    with a heaviness rising to heads
from urinal bowls, we had
Gagarin but Gagarin

also had us, every morning the same, a scraping
of sleeves over desks in the wake
of writing & every noon
the spoons would strike the hour, we had

table duty, milk duty, the force
   of emptiness in our eyes jelly
     in our ears until
it fell silent,
the force of gravity fell silent
     that was what hurt
     in our caps

when we peed in the windbreak trees,
when we spoke, we had
rote slogans: to our planet's shadow sides
    at least *we hold a light*
      first all together & then

            each of us silently
            in private once more. we had

no luck. so the houses fall down
                   and in the end we become
          small again &
ride back into the villages of wood, of
straw, the ones we came from, cracked & thin
with an echo whetted

on the wind: say hi to Gagarin from us, we
had no luck, the exit back
to our villages
                   & the villages' departure
over the fields by night . . .

Potemkin's village

at the cockle stove, dancing,
thinking about my dancing, I
   did my best, you swore
up a storm, spoke in weathervanes:

water hangs on the snow
there's weeping in the blood, stamping
after flakes, in the foot-stamps

a cross-hatching, a happy end
to the working day hangs behind the clocks
behind the clocks

a waft of time
& temperatures rising
once again; you
   lit the furnace every
day, I laughed

into the bread of this place
my head made heavy
I stopped in my tracks

while I spun and spun
   my eyes full of black

for Nadja

bugs

walking was ill in the eyes
frustrated the light
    of heavy bodies
lacking weight: winter till
        all goes black, little squirt,
        one just shut your mouths and sing
        two *incy wincy spider*
        climbed up the water spout three louder &

    we sang became
louder smaller black and disappeared
    were bugs and crept
down the throat into the echo of the institute

through waxy smells toilet bowls dis-
infections with the person in front down
the line stanza by stanza to the buckets
in the cellar every day we swallowed

    with our meals
the waiting bug on the wall yet
it grew we sang threw up began
our song again to strangle it on its back

slowly smaller louder singing yet
it grew had ears peed, God we
sang till blue-black in the face and disappeared were
bugs *four*: that was me.

my cheerfulness stood propped
in this dark hallway
leant with one cheek for
    walking was ill
      in the eyes frustrated
      the light of heavy bodies
      lacking weight . . .

brain dead Sunday

I count to myself, until I can sleep
they dialled me back quieter today
at one hundred the grass grows over the sheep
and then they're gone.

the blood's been washed, the breath pumped
he with his back full of pus
fixed to this chrome sky.
none is one, more alone than

the daily bread, give us
the liver, the kidney, the neck
   give us both
lungs' wings, for a river
runs over your shoulder out

of time: the lamb was slaughtered
God be with thee, a slit
in seven eyes
on a scalpel blade

over mountains, over steppe, ventured

our bold division but we
stood as if retched up
in front of every monument to an unknown someone. shoulder
to shoulder, half-swimmers, minute-takers
　　　paralysed before the broadly
cast namelessness
of our liberators. not the image, the

　　　grey-belt-&-garrison-cap, not
the metal border of my mirror, which
I recognised from
the time when the rain stood still
in the tree. for walking meant trotting, light
snowfall, in which fingers shimmered
frozen off at the trousers' seams, luminous every salute
　　　in its sequence
of crumbs and entrails. our greeting
with flat, raised hand, which came free, pointed
to birds standing hard in the wind, sparrows
in the brain, who went down, saluting.

each interpretation makes us
want to gag, with its interpreter
round its legs, whispering
is it or isn't it me

we always said hello we answered

even those birds come hungering
down from above
    & with our caps
we greeted the light

of each distance not understood
in the window the cherry calf
               the tree for sleep
                the tart
   the light was undisputed
a modest light
a thin warping
of the dark in the wind:

   who is ringing a bell this late
over the fields who is heading
into the woods? this way we grew old

& had to go back we welcomed
the gravity in our caps
in the open air we hoisted the horses

heavenwards we gave & knew
   the answer every day
     we hoisted the damp fear

on our hands over the desks we
threw our hands
    far beyond fear:

I crouched in Faraday's cage
beside the White Elster near Zwötzen
in the riverbed people said hello, they greeted
their shoes ruined for years . . .

grassland

Sundays the heavens are erased.
and on the sleepy anniversaries
of the deaths of the villages, they repeat
      the game: from the
clearing comes wind, wood

breathes, thank goodness, wood
thinks differently, and
      the ticking debris breathes
in the treetops, the leaves in the gravel
on the move in the shafts breathe, only

      those down there, who lie
just under, suck and hold
their breath,
little & stiff: and only then

you look like grass, bent hard
to earth, your gaze
the vacant blink of lashes . . .

my gems, my boat, my canvas gym bag

kindly enough they never
ignored me. quite the opposite,
may we smoke they said and
of course I said, we may
eat, drink, sleep, we must
while away the time somehow, these evenings
are long and one drinks one's
punch at home or elsewhere, owning a boat
      does lift the heart, and after all
one has an ashtray here and there
a shaver, yes, they smoke
but kindly enough
they keep their own
no less within their reach
      than I keep mine:
a little spilt on the table, always, how embarrassing,
more gone missing down the coat's lining, simply
careless, or that was promptly
forgotten once the daring
journey started. scarcely
am I
  underway before I think

how beautiful sheep are
what treasures
      scarcely am I
finally home again before
someone calls out to me, good sir
there's something on the ground and

if I weren't so small and weak
just once I'd have loved to ask:
is it my gems?
my boat?
my canvas gym bag?

dedicated to Hans Henny Jahnn

IV

in field Latin

once established we're bast
   under the bark
a guest behind rinds & inner child
of the roads leaving town. these

roads are a murmured
language, going past what used
to be said along the gardens
   towards field Latin. there

the child sits on a hill the
world is made of sand, murmured languages
roll inwards longing
also for water, bridges

    & roads
need softly
rolling languages your
own child in field Latin

Gera

you don't speak
      of the valleys and heights, the light
speaks of the Elster. but even outside
was something like inside
      under the window and down
the street the waving songs . . . I had

      a room with a recorder
group fleshy angels roared through
the treetops into the rafters *the dew*
sprang back into the air; if

we had not existed
      we would've had to
invent ourselves in the morning before leaving
      & paper
posted daily for stiffness
in the peaks of our caps: *inside*
a dreaming in the feet & outside if we didn't

      exist
the ebb would rise in the rain the waters
      would rise would blacken
the bogs the wild boar in the evening
the black of cinders would stand on the streets &
black elderberries of the various
blacks piled on umbels, on ulcers
      sought & the findings state: that around

time's neck we would have bound a weight

moss fire

. . . spoke at the stone for the unknown
who were laid aside; so many
the little Nazi herded along here
that they cursed their eyes
in the darkness . . . can you
make out your house & your
mother hung high with her feet
in the air, when you all
were sat round the table come evening; what

would you wish from her sleeping skeleton
– poppies & sweet grasses, lies
   will never lie for long . . .

Sundays I thought of God

Sundays I thought of God when we
would take the bus to tour our town.
by the fire pond by the road

a substation stood & forty-three
electric cables came from air into
this house of hard-baked brick; and there

in the house by the road God lived. I saw
how nested in electric
cable ends he squatted between brick

walls without a window there on the ground
in darkness by the road behind
a door of steel

the dear Lord would sit; he was
infinitely small & laughed
    or slept

Bols ballerina

I had a bottle of schnapps
with a prima ballerina her
right leg was stiff everything spun
around it and yet

she kicked the left one high
to her head as long
as the bottle's little song was
spoiling me but then

when the spring ran out it happened
that her swinging leg was left
in the air that the schnapps
    stood for, balanced

between her head and the bottom
of the bottle. trembling but
fixedly then the pale
little tip of her leg pointed
    at me.

born 'fourteen / name / sex

& date deceased . . . please
write that down, I counted
        the gut-rot, the shoe-tree, that's how
she cracked the sheep's drought of laughter, dancing, like the ash
        that rose from the trays of coal stoves
in Sunday-best rooms, she rubbed an echo
in her apron pockets, the dust and scree
of insects, in the dark, her fist

        at hand, the rhyme
on the wall set off her *wandering*, the
embankment set off
a putting of questions in the gravel: what

turns around at these footsteps, a body
jerking & bobbing towards what, it happens
over accordions, model trains &
        novels, post-war
plagues of slogans, *the transition
from ape to man*, import
                export of raisin
bombers, scarab beetles & American
potato bugs introduced by air: *everything*

had to be made up / upright, like how
a bird twists its neck, she
        left with hanging steps which
still pointed and ran from
the main house to the wings, over

the divided ceilings of her children's rooms animals &
    garages, straight
out of time

one o'clock on the towers

in the shadow of the *veranda*, meaning: rough plaster
under a felted roof, from there
the silence traced its course & rising from

the turf around the house
those might come who
we said to ourselves on clear

one o'clock Wednesday afternoons
                    had broken off
from the branches, a

thin, extenuated rustling
soon went from bird feet out
of the garden into the heat of this

lunch hour, while sirens might stand ringing
on the towers like Mussolini helmets
automatically unmanned . . .

stick boy

      that was the saw
dust smell:

a tree leant
on its man
who looks out
who looks at you and through
the cut of his face
   & out

of the tree the child peels himself:
that's how he stands
from outside there
with his own blood & his foundling voices

poetry is my gun dog

but the hare, maybe
he'll slip by? a zigzag, a mud track, beside it
   a big animal springs
out of the firebreak . . . but little
leads through the poem, something perhaps

in utter tiredness, rich
omens, leftovers, and
a tinge as the leaves unfurl on trees . . . the head

grows, the rooms
contract, paling fences and chevaux
de frise in the breach, the gun dog sings
old comrades, which in the poem means:
generations, who stumbled on with forward
ellipses, mechanical sniffing & tumbling, which means
tiny otters & their quickly scratched escape
to the rocks. in contrast the locust trees
of Theophrastus: unmoving until May. we
   realise that

we stand before it, while
time passes. a man
crosses the street with
an envelope in his hand & speaks
into the air. I said: perhaps

a zigzag, a mud track, how
   the images seep out
of a dead hare, until
he's blind, white, at the very bottom
of the urban signage hierarchy

for Peter Huchel

I'm tired

before bed I spoke softly to
my mother's hairpiece I
can't remember how

it sang on its pale
polystyrene head so softly
songs of Lorelei, it sang

once more to be
twenty & said that
I should get to bed

V

travel in the nineteen hundreds

I could still see light in
the lattice of the bridge I heard
the metals
    & baggage train how

    was the view out of
the drivers' cabs — long stretches long
    gazes? lovely when the machines
moved, the cuneiform
in bird-roads stood
still; the losses, briefly

    singing fires out of
ashes & salt in the transmission poles. then
    came the carriages endlessly
gentlemen rode to the gate they rolled like saws
        out into the tracks through

        the villages to the dance. there
they were the halls, that was
their patient black in the snow on the way & something
said without hands was sung. later carbide

    & bone haulage enormous
logistics lists which were pulled on the quiet,
over the golden bridge which would sway
    in the air's tonnage: *the first*

will be second . . . I'd
   rolled up close to it
my forehead closer still so that
my eyes were touching metal &
felt their lattice; I
   had only the question
of the tracks in mind: forwards
    & backwards

at night, among the noises

of the hamlet, when
the thing that looks out of your eyes
is still growing: yesterday's
          ashes, the cattle
leant with their breath
on our house's stonework; it

was my breadth, and even
standing back it's been said
   everyone remains

on their own: the fencing, the
shadows, the grass, the
lines of animal bodies in the dark, their
skeletons, the hermetic
turn of their hoofs and eyes, isolated,
and
their breath: isolated. I heard
a pleasure steamer on the canal, a trip

like a long body & rips in it, short
suspensions of breath, that's how
aviation develops

from navigation, also
     from the eyes
     of our ship we
and only we looked in: I
named the quiet
          at our feet compared
to the swaying of our heads

Black Africa, the knee, the

upper jaw *in nineteen hundred and fourteen* I asked, and
yes she said, but back home too
   the captain's standing, dead,
at the railing for her wheelchair, gazing
   into flowerbeds, he
shies away, his
feet are decorated
with a fish once
   she said that being loved
   requires an ungainly antelope gait
   in the river bed of a shoe, you get a glimpse

of just some steps by
   just one foot
in a shoe in Cameroon, and yes
   she said, whenever
   the barracks' damp
went through her, the hypnoses would begin
   hypnoses of the wood & hypnoses
   of the foxtrot, until
the chestnut bones would knock
in her dressing gown,
her seven watchdogs chained

and useless: just the white
of his hands brought
together in sleep, just
the plains & a man you see

stands within firing range before a man
within sight, behind them
a horse is flying
and swinging a rider, dead . . .

hers, for her man

the walking
   only the foul walking.
a wooden man . . . in Advent.
they're seeking a bed for the night
   over the marshes, he
   was still breathing
a long, a long-drawn tone, the

bubbles, in the bread, in the rain
   the bread all calcified
enough to make you cry, the song a
salty dog enough to make you cry, the
wooden man crying, he's
breathing still, the rain, a thin
tone in the air, we said

that the rattling came from the flag
but it was the man
& the woman on the bicycle
& their cart of tin, that

   was their song gone bad:
the sun breathes life into the stinking moon
the stinking moon breathes life into the steps the
steps of the man breathe life into the walking
   be a light . . .

citizen of the world

while we could now
unbuckle ourselves with a final silent jerk in
the net of meridians and latitudes, while the land

gains time underfoot behind
the dunes and grim woods and catches
its breath in the tropics' kitchens, where

the hyenas oxidise, green and mute
like the strangler fig trees in the ruins of Ta Prohm; I heard
as an apparently dead bird that had crashed

into the windowpane stumbled
to its feet in the sand and
for a second it was bright

in my room. I heard, under my feet, that something, a
grand solace, began to breathe, the same mute
entities that lie in houses

by motorways, wherever you go and knock,
they breathe it out, they are worms, dolls
chocolate boxes, at night

their windows fogged, the same
shivering in their eye sockets, clapping
of hands . . .

almost frosty still, yet

    from under
the telegraph poles' tar-taping the fresh
beetles scrabble to the light. legs splayed,
the birds are on them, the

    consumer majority, that's how you trundle
out, at noon, a silence
in the air, the net curtains, open a chink &
the crockery crashing / the whole

broken-through existence in April. even
out of the thick undergrowth other
    species push out
& grow. tiny
& mean, the silence
of eaten animals. the main thing is

little here leads to the poem. maybe
when the butcher's van calls. or
a man appears, who as he walks
vaporises again above
the street and
the light salts of his breath drift

over. *like*
    a wave-tossed boat, he caves
    into prayer, jesusmary let
me also look back
quick and see if right now
you're still there . . .

Castlegregory / Co. Kerry

yes it embodies it
hangs on the wall
walks backwards
gives milk, spilt, is also

       a movement
& the fly on it
embodies the light the light
is the unknown darker light
   into which the bushes

throw themselves come evening embodies the crypt
the wintry sea the long gaze
of children looking out embodies the lapa
loma before the adieu: the fly is throttled.

just the way things are

shame his arms were too short, they didn't quite reach
to his hands. his legs were really short too, shame, where

were his feet. shame the neck was *in itself* too short
the trunk, mr trunk, was too short for itself, he liked

having arms and legs, but shame he had to let them go
after the piano hands, after the dance feet, hack away —

good evening Cape

out here they love their
little crumpled-as-all-fuck dogs. and here it's
not as far
from the sofa to the fence
as in America. and in the evening
when the light goes out
up above, in the trees
a little crumpled-as-all-fuck shadow leans against the gate
and says:
out here I'm loved, you know, I'm loved

gravity

                            with distance
tougher signs arise. the leg
twitches in the dream, do you hear
         the leaves on the street, insects
on feet of clay. the old

leadership disappears, overturned, only
a twitching *inside*
the apparatus. the reeds
find their voice; tomorrow
the snakes will be straightened.

each poem moves slowly
from above to below, from below
to above, retains
its stubborn nature, which still
turns its burnt-out flower heads
towards the sun. the *I*
embodies itself, when it
throws off the covers
it grabs, in a beat, the heart
of the mummy. each poem
moves along ant streets
through the echo districts of its bell.

evenings we return home tired
the spider's leg
is still twitching, far off
from the limping rest. a trickle

on the windowpane and the clouds of locust trees,
turned to stone in the crack, close
everything up, the wind

centres us in the house, while we sleep, while
rolled up, squatting, we
    crawl back into
the ur-figures and what
still shoots out over our bent backs
onto snowed-in tracks. someone
wanted to check the water meter, someone

took the gas reading. the I
reads the iron counter
hanging in your veins: each poem
gnaws at the singing bone, at child's height
the poem is worn thin
and narrates

IV

VI

sixty-nine, old century

on wood the footsteps recall to themselves the darkness,
the hourly break, the bell that rang above the stairs, the slaps
on the nouns to salt our memory. crouched
& deafened behind the ears
    time stalled. from

a young age something
    was ready for later, always
        was true longer
            & earlier, the mnemonic
is the salt of
                broken birds behind the ears, so that

    the benches couldn't have
outlasted us, the inks, pale
    the cursing & scowling slumped
in salt hate stood
prepared, always prepared, above
the skirting board the cracks began, rivers

and conurbations, before the Urals
    metastases of plaster painted
    over with oil, beyond them
Kamchatka, hardened, calcified, all the way to

Sakhalin I stood
    facing the wall, so that
    Amu Darya & Syr Darya flowed, I described
Jamilia's crying, now explain

               how you
                     would have cried & what the plough is,
the real burden of the apparent doctrine
         the Sholokhov horse-collar
         round the neck, is it only a kerchief
         am I the new frontier
         are you my curse, anvil

or Korchagin, the sick
         and freezing hand was the skin
         on the wall & the whitewash & the force of gravity
pressed to my lips, alone & whispering:
                     dear wire dear God Mrs
                     Bakuski leave off, come on, a crying

                     goes off
into the stoves, off
through the wall, off
into the ashes above the courtyard, yet
         what is a crying, gravity
         went wrong, light
         misted against the light, the stars

rose onto
armoured gun carriages above the glass
on the glued window casements
out into the air
over the pact

sleep stood
prepared, always prepared & the *I*
         stood facing the wall, it
         was cool on my lips
         burnt, only
those who could have left
were driven out, now they came
silently back from the ships
up the tables
back to their salted
     files, they added

to the platform, the oil & the foreign world
   their burden, they added
      the way things go, the waiting
         with stupidity, the snowmelt
            with glances out into the dark
& the soil of
shame, which

finally scatter
     under stamping feet
     over the light well
     under yard duty
hope too stood prepared, always prepared,
an iron handrail

encircled the yard, the chestnut trees, the heads
flew with the slaps

back into the post-war,
    the creamy quark on steamed
        potatoes back into the first
flag assembly, traitors to the plough we went

round in circles, we
    encircled the milk
    in vessels for walking
    our steps scabbed over,
the flight
of a coarse, unnatural dark

closed off the vaulted roof at noon, laid
down on a woven stretcher, sleep
lay blinded beside our hands, all tagged
    with sweat:

they had trimmed the wick down.
and came in.
extinguished the light
    between their fingers; washbasins, next scene
& waking dream of figures of speech; steps to the window &
                                            twitching
        all the lace curtains, Mrs
            Bakuski must die, oh-ho, Mrs Bakuski
. . . we blind & silent under the covers

        coloured the shadows
        above the eyes, a

childish pus, the true blue
stayed shut in the corners, didn't
shame stand prepared, always prepared,
in the change of season
white chestnuts ripen in pockets, the lark

stabs Lark Sunday to death, the lamp
    in the gravel, the drinkers'
folk dress & their patios & bottles
matured in pockets, the stone

a promissory note: the bird
snuffed out mid-flight, its eye
stares at the heavens & in
    abandoned orbits

the dead nursery-school teacher circles, sleep, Hypnos,
    bitter shoe & satchel circle, bag & tin, the
    lunchbox circles, the gym bag
circles out there, sleep, Hypnos, circling

depressions lit up and lifting high
on coffee grounds, in the row of wash stations
    in the sheep's laughter
    there grew
another seventy barracks, meat-
batteries over the hills
    on the edge of night, is

the sleepy child now prepared, always prepared
he leans out, rickety
in the ruined enclosure
in his
playpen behind the times, half-

dirt, half-dead, fills lungs, once from the top, I am prepared:
 if the father pulls back his left
 he hits out, pulls back his right
 hits out, the child's
 head bowed, the mother
 shakes a little dream
 bloody from a little tree, look, me,
 at me, I'm talking to you
 with tears, with
 creation in the blood
   & all
the points of its crown bitten off.

TRANSLATOR'S NOTES

latrine

In November 1946 Günter Eich published the poem 'Latrine' in the German cultural newspaper *Der Ruf* (The Call). It begins so: 'Over a stinking ditch, / paper full of piss and blood, / surrounded by glistening flies, / I squat.' Eich's poem is one of the earliest and most radical of German responses to the war. It has been seen as the moment when post-war German literature was born. It also caused shock and scandal, not least because Eich rhymed *Urin* (urine) with the canonical poet Hölderlin, which led some defenders of Hölderlin to talk of the end of German literature. Like Eich's poem, Seiler's 'latrine' is a moment of sober stocktaking, looking back at a now finished period of history, and without any hint of *Ostalgie* (nostalgia for East Germany).

Greater Berlin, one

Regarding the 'bottles, first off heavy / and hard to let go, then empty / buried in rats' / holes, their necks whistling', Seiler wrote: 'There's a realistic method in the background here. People used to put bottles in mole holes with the necks facing into the wind, to cause a continual whistling sound that drove away the moles. My grandfather did that too, with all his schnapps bottles.'

spoilheap glow
In the Erzgebirge (Ore Mountains) and parts of the Ruhr, a common greeting when you see someone is *Glück auf!* Literally, the words mean: 'luck' and 'up'. It is the phrase, shortened centuries ago, with which miners wished each other good luck entering or leaving a mine, and the phrase then spread to be commonly used by all in the mining areas.

scissors knives and matches
This poem riffs on a German nursery rhyme about four dangerous things children shouldn't play with, 'Messer Gabel Schere Licht', knife, fork, scissors, matches. The rhyme also became a well-known 1965 pop song.

in the East, Lisa Rothe
This poem goes back to Seiler's memory of exploring long-abandoned flats in Gera's Untermhaus district, a district where the housing stock had become dilapidated. The 'Rothe' in the title is a not uncommon German surname, but it is pronounced the same as the colour red, which is *rot*, or *rote* if before a feminine noun.

Wismut is the name of the Russian–East German enterprise that was set up to mine uranium in the Communist era.

on the sheep track
The ending 'silence / is a vertical sleep' is from a Jan Skácel poem, as translated by the German poet Reiner Kunze in the poem 'Schlaf direkt gegenüber von uns', which appeared in the 1982 collection *Wundklee*. In Seiler's novel *Star 111*, the protagonist Carl says, 'The best thing Kunze ever did were his Skácel translations.'

but it was good
The 'sails / of our galleon-lamp' refer to a replica of Columbus's *Santa María* that had a light bulb inside and was a common fixture in homes in 1970s East Germany.

'Nails, alone / as Crusoe, crooked in slates' is a very oblique reference to the slate-walled houses in Seiler's Thuringian homeland, with some nails going in crooked or twisted.

It was part of the local miners' idiom to talk about going down into the mine as going to be baptised.

Berlin room
Found mainly in Berlin's multistory residential buildings, a 'Berlin room' is a courtyard-facing corner room located between the front or back and a side wing. They are often large, but as they have only one window, in the corner, they remain dark. They are also found in other places in Germany where similar building plans were used.

This poem moves around an interior, a flat, that bears the impression of the period around 1900 but which was changed and became somewhat run-down in the GDR era.

Good workers in the GDR were *Aktivisten* (Activists).

pitch & glint
The internet suggests that 'tree cake', *Baumkuchen*, is an elaborate kind of cake made by dripping the dough onto a spit so it forms rings from the centre. I hope to try it when I next go to Germany.

over mountains, over steppe, ventured
The start of this poem is from a revolutionary song that was much sung in East German schools. It was a Russian song, 'Po dolinam i po vzgoriam', much translated, and was also known as the 'Partisan's Song'.

grassland
This is a poem about Seiler's first home village, Culmitzsch, and the other nearby villages that were erased by the uranium mining.

my gems, my boat, my canvas gym bag
This poem takes its tone and mood from Hans Henny Jahnn's novel *Das Holzschiff* (translated into English as *The Ship*).

moss fire
The German poem's title, 'mossbrand' (a coinage combining 'moss' and 'fire') is also the title of a literary journal that Seiler co-founded and co-edited in the 1990s, *Moosbrand*. As he wrote to me: 'The word is an invention. Back then, because we needed a title for the journal, we went from *Moosband* (moss-bound, the journal's cover was that green-brown colour) to *Moosbrand*. Then there were a number of poems by different poets with that title.'

poetry is my gun dog
This poem is dedicated to Peter Huchel, in whose former house in Wilhelmshorst Seiler lives, and 'the locust trees / of Theophrastus' is a reference to a poem in Huchel's collection *Chausseen Chausseen*. You may also recognise it from Michael Hamburger's book of Huchel translations, *The Garden of Theophrastus*.

In Case of Loss, Seiler's non-fiction collection, contains two remarkable essays about Huchel's house and his notebook of images and phrases.

Castlegregory / Co. Kerry
'the lapa / loma before the adieu' is a child's mishearing of the name of a popular song and album from 1973. It is a reference that also pops up in *Star 111*, where we hear that someone 'looked like Mireille Mathieu on the *La Paloma, Adieu* album cover'.

good evening Cape
In the essay 'Under the Pine Vault' (*In Case of Loss*), Seiler says,
'As an initial image of our new home, *Cape Cod Evening* by
Edward Hopper seemed about right. [. . . The painting's] forest
behind the house did not remind me of our forest, yet the image
still reminded me of our new home, of a kind of easeful absence
that I recognised in the man and that gesture he is making by
reaching out his hand. That attentive, abstracted look, which can
bring poems into being, turned "Cape Cod" into "Cape Good"
and that became "good evening Cape", the title of the first poem
I wrote while living "out" in Wilhelmshorst. In this unfamiliar
Brandenburg landscape, among people who were strangers to
me and who did not greet each other on the street, I was able to
write in a way that I had never managed in the city. I felt at home
from the very first day.'

sixty-nine, old century
Jamilia (also *Jamila* in English) is the 1958 novel by Chingiz
Aitmatov (also Aytmatov). A famous love story set in the Kyrgyz
steppes, it was a set text in East German schools.

MEMORY SALT

A Translator's Afterword

The factual, the concrete, only deserves its place in the text as a means of supplying atmosphere or providing the grounding for its delicate structure. This means that nothing ought to remain merely biographical in the narrow sense. It is never a question of 're-creation'. [. . .] Objects are not important for their past reality, but as part of our perception, of hearing or seeing, of the very sensations they once helped to shape. They are the go-betweens and indirect paths taking you to the poem.

LUTZ SEILER

from 'The Tired Territory'

(*In Case of Loss*, translated by Martyn Crucefix)

My first experience of Seiler's childhood region – the Erzgebirge, or 'Ore Mountains', in the south of what had been East Germany – came when I stayed with a pen pal in a small town there in the summer of 1990. The currency had just been converted and the local television station was running a list of all the street name changes on loop, as Communist references were quickly erased. Less than a decade later I moved to Dresden, to a flat in an old, unrenovated house. Heated, as so many were, by a six-foot-high tiled cockle oven, every morning in winter there was the trip to the cellar for a bucket of coal. On the stairs I'd pass Frau —, slow on her feet, who had lived in the house since her childhood, when she sheltered in the cellar during the 1945 firebombing. Next to the house were the allotments, where we newcomers were barely tolerated, because we didn't plant enough vegetables, as all the older East Germans continued to do religiously, though by then perhaps more as an excuse for time spent pottering and drinking in the gardens. Just in front, while we lived there, the cobblestone road was tarred over. I've never felt the distinct layers of history so simultaneously present as when I lived in the former East Germany.

Lutz Seiler was born in 1963. His family lived in a region of the Erzgebirge where some of the world's largest deposits of uranium ore were being extracted by the Soviet Russian powers with brutal disregard for the environment or human health. His grandfather was a miner, and could make the radio crackle with a wave of his hand. In 1968, Seiler's family and the rest of the village of Culmitzsch were evacuated, having been literally undermined. They moved to the nearby village of Korbussen, and then to Gera, the nearest town.

Time and place are essential to Seiler's atmosphere in this collection, though he doesn't evoke anything by straightforward means. Time and place set in motion a subjective vibration, an energetic headiness, which as a translator I had to access by tuning in to my own frequencies and associations. The East German settings and references can be translated, as long as the atmosphere is invisibly signalled, made transmissible, made to spark somehow.

This, combined with the fact that on a technical level Seiler's poetry is punchy, compressed and wholly its own thing, made the task of translation stretch into years. He is led by his ear, and his sound patterning and rhythmic, propulsive lines knit surreal and cryptic elements together. The focus pulls in and out, the cuts come quick, words shift into neologisms and pivot forward and backwards, pulling double duty in overlapping phrases.

How did I approach its translation? Sound came first, as it does in Seiler's composition. The poems had to have rhythm and sound patterning, more than literal sense equivalence. Word choices are sometimes about the resonances of a word across the collection, or indeed across his writing. There are also plenty of specific, though not immediately apprehensible, references to the times and places he draws on, about which I asked many questions, both of Seiler and of friends. I felt the need to understand the half-stated allusions and see 'the grounding' – the hidden geology – of the poems, so that no matter how little the landscape might be visible in the poem, when the fog lifts, it is there. I also tended to follow my nose rather than a set theoretical approach. In 'bugs', set in a brutal primary school, the poem quotes from a well-known German children's song about a bug waiting on the wall. Since in English we have 'Incy Wincy Spider' instead, I used that. Here it seemed more important to convey the school atmosphere than to be accurate about German children's songs. In 'spoilheap glow' I left in the German regional greeting of *Glück auf!* (literally: Luck up!), and added an endnote, partly because the poem itself describes the sound of the greeting as 'the little / spasm', and partly because I find it fascinating that this miner's greeting had become the everyday hello in this part of the world. As so often, each choice was also about finding the words to fit the rhythm.

The final poem, 'sixty-nine, old century', might be illustrative. In the first stanza there is a *Merksalz*, Seiler's neologism. *Merk* is about remembering and *Salz* is salt. It twists away by one letter from the German word for mnemonic, *Merksatz* (literally: remembering phrase). By altering that word, Seiler's new word talks about the workings of memory: salt preserves, intensifies flavours, and stings. The word *Salz* returns in the tenth stanza, as part of the proper noun *Salzgitter*. Salzgitter is a town. This is not common knowledge to Germans these days, but Seiler mentioned to me that the Central Registry of State Judicial Administrations had been established in Salzgitter, West Germany, in the aftermath of the construction of the Berlin Wall. Until its closure in 1992, its function was to verify human rights violations by the government of East Germany, such as the murder of East Germans trying to escape across the border. And yet, given how important salt is in this poem, and how unknown this government body would be to most readers, in English or German, I decided to give a translation that makes sure we don't lose in English this last mention of salt: '. . . up the tables / back to their salted / files'.

The book's original title, *pech & blende*, takes the German word for the radioactive ore uraninite and splits it in two. (Uraninite was formerly called pitchblende in English, from the German.) *Pech* means both tar (pitch) and bad luck, and *Blende* suggests something dazzling, shining or blinding. And there's the assonance of the phrase. The title perfectly embodies Seiler's capacity to hold together apparent opposites – the mystical and the manual, the rural and the industrial – as well as the sheer impossibility of doing his poems justice at every turn. I oscillated for years between four options and even considered a split title listing them all. In the end, I went for a title that had the dark and light of the original, its materiality and points of light, and also its assonance.

The English publication of *Pitch & Glint* comes twenty-three years after its original publication and yet now, with Russia's attempt to annex Ukraine, the period that it evokes is closer to us than ever. What happens in the past is rarely actually 'in the past' and, like uranium with its long half-life, harm lingers for generations. Lutz Seiler's poetry asks, among other things, how to remember. In the words of German poet Michael Krüger:

> Seiler is the odd one out, who can't and won't fit in; the loner who notices something on the way, who is blocked by something that puts itself in his way. His language is like that too: it feels its way forward, stops, stumbles, keeps going. It doesn't want to arrive, and has no destination. That keeps it nimble. *Pitch & Glint* was an event, because all of us who still believe poetry can do something, felt that something was being given voice by this poet, something that would otherwise have been hopelessly lost. (*Atelier*, 2003, volume 30, *Giovane poesia europea*; translation mine)

This book has benefited from the direct and indirect help of many people whom I'd like to thank. The poets, including Volker Sielaff, who gathered in Lesezeichen bookshop, Dresden, on Saturday afternoons over fresh pastries and owner Jörg Nollau's coffee. That was where I first heard Seiler's poems read and where I bought *pech & blende*. The German-language reviewers of *Star 111* who brought Seiler back to my attention at just the right moment, when, in the early days of the pandemic, I sorely needed a lodestar. Suhrkamp's Nora Mercurio, for entrusting three important books to And Other Stories. The translations of Seiler's poetry by Ken Babstock, Susan Bernofsky, Alexander Booth, Martyn Crucefix, Andrew Duncan, Sophie Duvernoy, Tony Frazer, Hans-Christian Oeser & Gabriel Rosenstock, and Andrew Shields, which often opened up lines and approaches for me. Gunter, my friend and one-time pen pal in Thalheim, who has kindly let me phone him now and then with questions as I've translated. Tara Tobler. The poems have gained immeasurably from her encouragement, suggestions and good-humoured editing. My absolute deepest thanks to her, too, for the many

Saturday mornings she's given me to go back to translation while she kept two, then three, feisty children entertained, not seldom outside on typically bleak Yorkshire days of wind and rain. And Lutz himself – I cannot thank him enough for answering my many questions with real frankness and for giving me the freedom to find the right words that work in English. Not that I haven't failed my editor and my poet at times. Any lapses are mine. Feel free to let me know about them. Thanks for reading.

STEFAN TOBLER

Edale, March 2023

In Case
of Loss

Lutz Seiler

&

¶ Before work every morning, I walk around outside the house. I look at the bark on a pine tree or at a patch of grass. I stand beside the garage, or I gaze back towards the house from the rear, from the margins of the forest, and I am hardly present. ¶ *Translated by Martyn Crucefix*

Star 111

Lutz Seiler

&

¶ The sight of his three worn mattresses on the floor, bound together with rope, the broken black-and-white television at the head of his bed and the soot-covered sheets hanging at the window and the coal box near the oven: it may have all been shabby and squalid, but it was full of promise, all these decrepit things [and the half-dilapidated building] all expressed the future. ¶ *Translated by Tess Lewis* ¶ Winner of an English PEN Award

Dear readers,

As well as relying on bookshop sales, And Other Stories relies on subscriptions from people like you for many of our books, whose stories other publishers often consider too risky to take on.

Our subscribers don't just make the books physically happen. They also help us approach booksellers, because we can demonstrate that our books already have readers and fans. And they give us the security to publish in line with our values, which are collaborative, imaginative and 'shamelessly literary'.

All of our subscribers:

- receive a first-edition copy of each of the books they subscribe to
- are thanked by name at the end of our subscriber-supported books
- receive little extras from us by way of thank you, for example: postcards created by our authors

BECOME A SUBSCRIBER, OR GIVE A SUBSCRIPTION TO A FRIEND

Visit andotherstories.org/subscriptions to help make our books happen. You can subscribe to books we're in the process of making. To purchase books we have already published, we urge you to support your local or favourite bookshop and order directly from them – the often unsung heroes of publishing.

OTHER WAYS TO GET INVOLVED

If you'd like to know about upcoming events and reading groups (our foreign-language reading groups help us choose books to publish, for example) you can:

- join our mailing list at: andotherstories.org
- follow us on Twitter: @andothertweets
- join us on Facebook: facebook.com/AndOtherStoriesBooks
- admire our books on Instagram: @andotherpics
- follow our blog: andotherstories.org/ampersand